52 WEEK DEVOTIONAL
FOR THE HEART OF A FATHER

Copyright © 2025 The Adventures of Pookie LLC
All rights reserved. This book or any portion thereof may not be reproduced or used in any manner whatsoever without the express written permission of the publisher except for the use of brief quotations in a book review.

For Bulk Order requests email: contact@adventuresofpookie.com

Printed in the United States of America
Paperback ISBN : 979-8-9988824-4-9
Hardcover ISBN: 979-8-9988824-5-6

www.AdventuresOfPookie.com

DEDICATION

To my father, Robert. Your love and guidance have been a constant source of inspiration throughout my life. You worked tirelessly to give us an incredible life, and in doing so, you passed down a deep appreciation for music and art that has shaped the way I see the world. Through both triumphs and challenges, your steady love and selfless sacrifices revealed to me the true heart of Christ-like service. I would not be the woman I am today without your unwavering support, your encouragement, and your example.

To my bonus dad, Bob. Your heart for others shines brightly in all you do. The way you love your family—and your bonus family—with gentleness and generosity has taught me what it means to love unconditionally. Your support has been a gift I never expected but will always treasure. I'm deeply grateful for your presence in my life.

To my father-in-law, Ken. You are a remarkable man whose love knows no limits. From the very beginning, you welcomed me into your family with open arms and an open heart. Your kindness, faithfulness, and devotion to those you love have blessed me more than words can say. I am honored to be part of your family.

INTRODUCTION

Fatherhood is one of the greatest callings a man can receive—and one of the most challenging.

It's not just about providing or protecting. It's about shaping hearts, building character, and reflecting God's love in everyday moments. From midnight feedings to tough conversations, from first steps to college goodbyes, the role of a father is sacred, significant, and never quite finished.

Yet in the pressure to be strong, reliable, and always "on," it's easy for a dad's heart to be overlooked—especially his need for encouragement, wisdom, and spiritual strength.

That's what this devotional is all about.

Strength to Lead: Devotions for the Heart of a Father is a 52-week journey designed to meet you in the real moments of fatherhood. Whether you're in the early years or parenting adults, these devotions offer honest encouragement, biblical truth, and practical prayers to help you lead your family with courage, humility, and faith.

You don't have to have all the answers. You don't have to be perfect. But you do have access to the One who is.

God has entrusted you with this role—not

because you're flawless, but because He walks with you. His strength fills your weakness. His grace covers your mistakes. His wisdom equips your leadership.

So take a few quiet minutes each week to pause, reflect, and reconnect with your Heavenly Father. Let Him speak to your heart, renew your spirit, and remind you: you are not alone—and you are more equipped than you think.

You have the strength to lead. And it starts here.

THE STRENGTH BEHIND THE ROLE

SCRIPTURE

"But the Lord stood at my side and gave me strength..." — 2 Timothy 4:17 (NIV)

DEVOTIONAL

Fatherhood can feel like standing in the middle of a storm, holding your family steady while the winds of life howl around you. There are bills to pay, choices to make, and hearts to shepherd. You're expected to lead with wisdom, protect with courage, and love with patience. It's a noble calling—but a heavy one.

But here's the truth: You were never meant to carry that weight alone.

Paul, in his final letter to Timothy, speaks of a moment when everyone else abandoned him. Yet he wasn't crushed. Why? *"The Lord stood at my side and gave me strength."* That same promise is for you. You don't have to be strong enough on your own. Your strength to lead doesn't come from performance or perfection—it comes from presence. God's presence. He stands beside you.

Each decision you face today, each challenge

that comes your way—face it with the confidence that you are not leading your family alone. God is with you. You lead best when you lead from that place of dependence on Him.

PRAYER

Father, thank You for standing beside me. Remind me daily that I don't have to lead alone. Give me the strength, humility, and wisdom to guide my family in Your ways. Help me rely on You more than myself. Amen.

REFLECTION

Where have I been trying to lead in my own strength? What would it look like to invite God into that area today?

_____
_____
_____
_____
_____
_____
_____
_____

LEADING BY EXAMPLE

SCRIPTURE

"Set an example for the believers in speech, in conduct, in love, in faith and in purity."
— 1 Timothy 4:12 (NIV)

DEVOTIONAL

Kids are always watching. More than we realize, they are observing how we speak to others, how we handle stress, how we respond to setbacks, and how we navigate the daily ups and downs of life. From the way we treat strangers to the way we apologize when we're wrong, our children are learning what it means to live with integrity, compassion, and courage. Even in the quiet moments, they are soaking in the values we demonstrate. They may not always repeat what we say—but they will often imitate what we do.

That's why leadership in the home isn't about having all the right answers or being perfect. It's about modeling a life anchored in Christ—day in and day out. When your words and actions consistently reflect your faith, you give your children something powerful: a living, breathing example of what it means to follow Jesus. They begin to understand that faith isn't just a Sunday activity; it's a daily commitment. Your example may very well become the foundation they stand on when life tests their own faith.

PRAYER

Lord, help me lead by example today. Let my words and actions reflect Your love and truth. Make me a father who inspires faith by the way I live. Amen.

REFLECTION

What are three recent moments when my actions reflected Christ to my children—and one moment where I could have responded differently? What might God be inviting me to change or strengthen in my daily example?

_____
_____
_____
_____
_____
_____
_____

GRACE FOR IMPERFECT FATHERS

SCRIPTURE

"But he said to me, 'My grace is sufficient for you, for my power is made perfect in weakness.'"
— 2 Corinthians 12:9 (NIV)

DEVOTIONAL

You're going to mess up. You'll lose your temper, say something you regret, miss an important moment, or fall short in ways that weigh on your heart. It's part of being human—and part of being a father. The pressure to get everything right can feel overwhelming, but the truth is, perfection was never the expectation. Your children don't need a flawless dad; they need a faithful one.

Your mistakes don't disqualify you. In fact, how you handle failure might teach your kids more than your success ever could. When you own your shortcomings, ask for forgiveness, and keep showing up, you're modeling humility, resilience, and the power of grace. These are lessons they'll carry for life.

The strength to lead doesn't come from pretending to have it all together. It comes from staying rooted in God, trusting that His grace is enough to cover your weakness, and believing that He's working in you—even on the hardest days. Let your dependence on Him be the greatest example you give your children.

PRAYER

Father, I fall short so often. Thank You for loving me anyway. Help me receive Your grace and extend it to my children. Make Your strength visible in my weakness. Amen.

REFLECTION

Think of a recent moment when you fell short as a dad. How did you respond—and what might you do differently next time with God's help? Write a short prayer asking God to use even your failures to shape your children and strengthen your leadership.

_____
_____
_____
_____
_____
_____
_____

TIME IS THE TREASURE

SCRIPTURE

"Teach us to number our days, that we may gain a heart of wisdom." — Psalm 90:12 (NIV)

DEVOTIONAL

The days can feel long, especially when you're juggling work, responsibilities, and the everyday demands of fatherhood. But when you look back, you'll realize how quickly the years have passed. Time seems to slip away faster than we expect, and the moments that felt ordinary are the ones your children will cherish most.

The best gift you can give them isn't the latest gadget or the perfect birthday gift—it's your time. Every shared meal, every bedtime story, every walk together creates memories that will last a lifetime. Your presence matters more than you might realize. It's in those small, seemingly insignificant moments that trust is built, hearts are nurtured, and the foundation for a lasting relationship is laid.

Don't underestimate the power of simply being there. Your consistency in showing up, day after day, teaches your children what love, commitment, and faithfulness truly look like. These moments are the ones that shape their hearts for years to come.

PRAYER

Lord, help me value the time I've been given. Teach me to be present with my children and to invest my time in ways that truly matter. Amen.

REFLECTION

Think about a recent moment when you were fully present with your children. How did that time impact your relationship with them? What can you do this week to intentionally give them more of your time and attention, even in the midst of your busy schedule?

_____
_____
_____
_____
_____
_____
_____
_____
_____

A LEGACY OF FAITH

SCRIPTURE

"The righteous man walks in his integrity; his children are blessed after him." — Proverbs 20:7 (NKJV)

DEVOTIONAL

You're not just raising kids; you're shaping the future. Every decision you make, every action you take, and every lesson you teach is laying the foundation for who your children will become. They are watching, learning, and absorbing everything you do, and those lessons go far beyond childhood. What you instill in them now will echo through their lives, their families, and even future generations.

A father who walks in integrity, keeps his word, and follows Jesus faithfully is building more than memories. He's building a legacy. The example you set today doesn't just shape the way your children live—it influences how they will lead, love, and serve others. When you live with purpose and authenticity, your children learn what it means to be men and women of character and faith.

This legacy isn't about perfection; it's about faithfulness. By choosing to walk with integrity and trust in God, you're creating a ripple effect that can impact your children and their children for years to come. You are leaving behind more than a family; you're leaving a legacy that points to eternity.

PRAYER

God, give me the strength to live with integrity. Let the legacy I leave be one that points my children to You. Help me walk the path today that I want them to follow tomorrow. Amen.

REFLECTION

Reflect on the legacy you want to leave behind. What are the key values and qualities you want to pass on to your children? How can you take practical steps today to begin building that legacy, even in the small, everyday moments?

_____

_____

_____

_____

_____

_____

_____

THE POWER OF A FATHER'S WORDS

SCRIPTURE

"The tongue has the power of life and death, and those who love it will eat its fruit."
— Proverbs 18:21 (NIV)

DEVOTIONAL

Your words carry incredible weight. As a father, the things you say to your children have the power to shape their self-image, their confidence, and even their future. A single word of encouragement can uplift them, while a careless remark can leave a lasting wound. It's easy to underestimate the impact of what we say, but our words can either build up or tear down the hearts of those we love most.

Are your words building your child's confidence or planting seeds of doubt? Speaking life means choosing to affirm, encourage, and correct in love. It's about intentionally speaking truth that reflects God's love for them—affirming their worth, acknowledging their efforts, and gently guiding them when they fall short. When you speak with grace and wisdom, you're creating a safe space for your children to grow.

What you say to your children doesn't just affect the moment—it becomes part of their inner dialogue. Over time, your words form the voice they hear in their heads as they navigate the world. Make sure that voice is one of blessing, encouragement, and truth. You have the power to shape their identity by the words you speak.

PRAYER

Lord, help me to speak life over my children. Let my words reflect Your truth and grace. Teach me to use my voice to encourage, guide, and love well. Amen.

REFLECTION

Think about the words you've spoken to your children recently. Are there moments where your words have built them up or torn them down? What is one specific thing you can say today to encourage or affirm your child, helping them feel valued and loved?

_____
_____
_____
_____
_____
_____

FAITH OVER FEAR

SCRIPTURE

"When I am afraid, I put my trust in you."
— Psalm 56:3 (NIV)

DEVOTIONAL

Fatherhood can be a journey filled with fear—fear of failing as a parent, fear for your children's safety, fear of not being enough. These worries can weigh heavy, especially when you feel the responsibility of shaping their futures. It's natural to want to protect them and guide them well, but the fears that come with fatherhood can sometimes feel overwhelming, making it hard to know where to turn.

But God invites you to exchange those fears for faith. Faith doesn't require ignoring the challenges or pretending the hard things aren't real. It means trusting that God is with you every step of the way—through the sleepless nights, the difficult decisions, and the uncertainties that life throws at you. When you place your trust in Him, you can lead your family with the assurance that He's holding both you and your children in His hands, even when you don't have all the answers.

Choosing faith over fear doesn't make the challenges disappear, but it empowers you to face them with the confidence that God's presence is enough. When fear rises, let it be a prompt to pray and trust in God's perfect provision for you and your family.

PRAYER

God, when fear rises in me, remind me that You are bigger than anything I face. Help me trust You with my children, my home, and my future. Strengthen my faith today. Amen.

REFLECTION

What fears do you find yourself carrying as a father? How can you release those fears to God and trust in His provision and guidance? Write a prayer asking for the courage to lead with faith, even when fear tries to take over.

_____

_____

_____

_____

_____

_____

A HEART THAT LISTENS

SCRIPTURE

"Everyone should be quick to listen, slow to speak and slow to become angry." — James 1:19 (NIV)

DEVOTIONAL

Sometimes, the most loving thing you can do as a dad is simply to stop and listen. In the busyness of life, it's easy to brush off a conversation or think that you already know what your child needs. But whether your child is four or fourteen, giving them your full attention communicates something powerful: "You matter." When you listen, you're not just hearing words—you're showing your child that their thoughts, feelings, and experiences are valued.

Listening allows you to lead with empathy rather than assumptions. It opens the door to understanding what's really going on in your child's heart and mind. When you listen well, you can guide with more wisdom and respond in a way that speaks directly to their needs, rather than just reacting out of impatience or frustration.

A listening heart creates a bridge to your child's world. It helps them feel seen and heard, fostering a deeper connection and trust between you. When they know you're genuinely listening, they're more likely to open up in the future and feel secure in your relationship.

PRAYER

Father, help me to be quick to listen and slow to speak. Teach me to hear my children's hearts, not just their words. Use my listening to build trust and connection. Amen.

REFLECTION

Reflect on a recent conversation with your child. How did you listen—or how could you have listened better? What is one way you can be more present and intentional in listening to your child today, without distractions?

_____
_____
_____
_____
_____
_____
_____
_____

WORK AS WORSHIP

SCRIPTURE

"Whatever you do, work at it with all your heart, as working for the Lord..." — Colossians 3:23 (NIV)

DEVOTIONAL

Whether you're clocking in at the office, fixing something around the house, or folding laundry, your work matters to God. It's easy to think of work as just a task to get done, but when done with a heart of service, it becomes an act of worship. The way you approach your responsibilities reflects your values and your faith. Each moment you dedicate to your work is an opportunity to honor God, not just to earn a paycheck.

Your children are watching how you handle the everyday tasks, big and small. They notice your attitude toward work—whether you do it with joy, excellence, or a sense of duty. Let your effort, no matter how mundane, reflect the One you serve. By showing your children the importance of integrity, diligence, and a heart that honors God, you teach them to approach their own responsibilities with the same mindset.

PRAYER

Lord, help me to see my work—whatever it is—as worship. Let my effort be honest, my attitude be grateful, and my example be strong. Amen.

REFLECTION

Think about how you approach your work, both at home and at your job. Do you do it as an act of service to God, or does it sometimes feel like a burden? How can you shift your perspective to approach your responsibilities with a heart of worship and integrity today?

_____
_____
_____
_____
_____
_____
_____
_____
_____
_____

THE GIFT OF FORGIVENESS

SCRIPTURE

"Be kind and compassionate to one another, forgiving each other, just as in Christ God forgave you." — Ephesians 4:32 (NIV)

DEVOTIONAL

Sometimes, the hardest part of being a dad isn't just forgiving others—it's forgiving yourself. We all make mistakes, but it's easy to let guilt and shame linger, especially when you feel like you've let your children down. Asking for forgiveness, whether from your kids or from God, requires humility and strength. It's about acknowledging that you're not perfect, but you're willing to grow and make things right.

Forgiveness is one of the most powerful lessons you can teach your children. When you apologize, you show them that grace isn't just something we receive, but something we extend to others. By admitting your mistakes and starting fresh, you model humility, accountability, and the power of moving forward. Far from a sign of weakness, this is true strength in action—the kind of leadership that leaves a lasting impact.

PRAYER

God, thank You for forgiving me through Christ. Help me be quick to forgive, and humble enough to ask for forgiveness when I need to. Let our home be full of grace. Amen.

REFLECTION

Is there a moment as a father that you still feel guilt or regret over? What would it look like to bring that to God and ask for His forgiveness—and if needed, your child's? Write a short prayer asking for healing and the courage to lead with humility and grace moving forward.

_____

_____

_____

_____

_____

_____

_____

_____

_____

PRAYING FOR YOUR CHILDREN

SCRIPTURE

"The prayer of a righteous person is powerful and effective." — James 5:16b (NIV)

DEVOTIONAL

There is no greater legacy you can leave your children than a life saturated in prayer. You won't always have the wisdom to know what to do or the power to shield your children from every hardship, but you have direct access to the God who does. In moments of uncertainty, fear, or joy, your prayers become a lifeline—lifting your children into the hands of the One who loves them even more than you do.

Prayer isn't just something you add to your parenting—it is a central part of it. When you pray over your children, you are fighting for their hearts, their futures, and their faith in ways unseen. Those quiet prayers you whisper before dawn, in the car, or beside their bed may seem small, but they echo into eternity. You may never see the full impact now, but your faithful intercession is shaping the course of their lives in powerful ways.

PRAYER

Father, thank You for the gift of my children. I lift them up to You. Guard their hearts, guide their paths, and draw them close to You. Help me be faithful in prayer, every day. Amen.

REFLECTION

What specific hopes or concerns do you have for your children right now? Take a few moments to write out a prayer for each child by name, entrusting them to God's care and asking Him to guide their steps, shape their hearts, and strengthen your role as their father.

_____
_____
_____
_____
_____
_____
_____
_____
_____
_____

TEACHING THROUGH TRIALS

SCRIPTURE

"Consider it pure joy… whenever you face trials of many kinds, because you know that the testing of your faith produces perseverance."
— James 1:2-3 (NIV)

DEVOTIONAL

Your kids are watching more closely than you think—especially when life gets tough. They see how you respond when things go wrong, when plans fall apart, or when stress is high. In those moments, you have a powerful opportunity: to either react with fear and frustration or to respond with faith and trust in God. Your reactions to the hard stuff speak louder than any words you say about faith.

When you walk through trials with grace—leaning on God, staying steady in your character, and choosing kindness even when it's difficult—you give your children a living example of what it means to be anchored in Christ. You show them that storms may come, but they don't have to shake your foundation. These moments don't just build your own faith; they are shaping the faith of the next generation watching you.

PRAYER

Lord, help me see trials as opportunities to grow in faith and to model trust for my children. Use every struggle to shape me—and them—into people of perseverance. Amen.

REFLECTION

Think about a recent challenge or stressful moment your family experienced. How did you respond, and what might your children have learned from watching you? How can you model a deeper trust in God the next time hardship arises?

_____
_____
_____
_____
_____
_____
_____
_____
_____

BEING PRESENT IN THE SMALL MOMENTS

SCRIPTURE

"Rejoice with those who rejoice; mourn with those who mourn." — Romans 12:15 (NIV)

DEVOTIONAL

You don't need a special occasion or a grand gesture to make a lasting impact—real fatherhood is built in the ordinary, everyday moments. It's found in the giggles over spilled cereal, the patience to listen to a rambling story, or the gentle response to a bad day. These moments may feel small or insignificant at the time, but they are the very places where trust and connection are built. They are the quiet threads that weave a strong and lasting bond between you and your child.

When you show up emotionally and mentally—not just physically—you're saying something powerful to your kids: "You matter. I see you. I'm here for you." These small acts of attention and affection assure them of their worth and security. Over time, they come to understand love not as a rare event but as a steady presence. And that presence will echo in their hearts for years to come.

PRAYER

Jesus, slow me down today. Help me pay attention to what matters most. Let me reflect Your love in the ordinary, unnoticed moments of fatherhood. Amen.

REFLECTION

Think back on one simple, everyday moment you shared with your child recently—a meal, a conversation, a bedtime routine. How did that moment strengthen your bond? What is one small, intentional way you can show up more fully for your child this week?

DISCIPLINING WITH LOVE

SCRIPTURE

"The Lord disciplines those he loves…"
— Hebrews 12:6a (NIV)

DEVOTIONAL

Discipline isn't about asserting control or demanding perfection—it's about guiding your children toward what is right and good. Just as God lovingly corrects His children to protect them and help them grow, your role as a father includes setting boundaries that teach your kids how to thrive. Discipline should never come from a place of anger or impatience, but from a heart that wants the best for your child, both now and in the future.

When you discipline with consistency, grace, and love, you mirror the heart of the Father. Your correction becomes a tool not for punishment, but for growth—helping your children understand consequences, take responsibility, and learn from their mistakes. Done well, discipline doesn't drive a wedge between you and your child—it builds trust, because they know you care enough to lead them with truth and love.

PRAYER

Father, help me discipline with wisdom, patience, and love. Let my correction teach my children, not just punish them. Use my leadership to point them to You. Amen.

REFLECTION

Think about your approach to discipline. Are there times when it comes from frustration rather than love? What would it look like to correct your children the way God corrects you—with patience, grace, and purpose? Write a prayer asking for wisdom and a heart that reflects God's love as you guide your children.

_____

_____

_____

_____

_____

_____

_____

_____

RESTING IN YOUR IDENTITY

SCRIPTURE

"See what great love the Father has lavished on us, that we should be called children of God!"
— 1 John 3:1a (NIV)

DEVOTIONAL

Before you carry the weight of being a father, provider, protector, or role model, remember this foundational truth: you are first and foremost a son—a beloved child of God. Your value isn't measured by how much you accomplish or how well you lead your family. It's grounded in your identity as His. When you know who you belong to, you can lead your children not from pressure or performance, but from a place of peace and purpose.

God's love for you is not something you have to earn or strive for—it's already yours. That unconditional love becomes the wellspring from which you parent. When you rest in your identity as His son, you can offer grace more freely, lead with humility, and love your children without fear of failure. Let the love you've received from your Heavenly Father shape the way you father your children today.

PRAYER

God, remind me that I am first and always Your child. Help me father my kids from a place of peace, not pressure. Let Your love be the foundation of my identity and my leadership. Amen.

REFLECTION

Take a moment to reflect on your identity as a child of God. How does this truth impact the way you father your children? What can you do today to lead from a place of peace and assurance in God's love rather than from pressure or perfection?

_____

_____

_____

_____

_____

_____

_____

_____

_____

A SERVANT LEADER

SCRIPTURE

"Whoever wants to become great among you must be your servant." — Matthew 20:26 (NIV)

DEVOTIONAL

True leadership in the kingdom of God flips the world's view of authority on its head. It's not about wielding power or control; it's about serving others in humility and love. Jesus, the ultimate example of leadership, led with a towel and a basin, demonstrating that the greatest leaders are those who are willing to serve. As a father, your leadership is defined not by what you command, but by how you serve. The small, unseen acts of love—whether it's making breakfast, giving a listening ear, or cleaning up after a long day—are where true leadership is formed.

Serving your family in these quiet moments might not earn praise or recognition, but it reflects the heart of Christ. Changing diapers, washing dishes, or staying up late to help with homework isn't a sign of weakness; it's a powerful display of love and strength. These actions, though often unnoticed, are the backbone of fatherhood, building trust, nurturing your children's hearts, and teaching them the value of serving others. In God's kingdom, this kind of service is not just honorable; it is the very essence of leadership.

PRAYER

Jesus, You served with humility and love. Help me lead my family the same way. Make me a servant first, and a leader second. Let my actions speak louder than my words. Amen.

REFLECTION

Think about the ways you serve your family in the everyday moments. How does it feel to lead through service, even when it goes unnoticed? What are some simple acts of service you can do today to model Christ-like leadership for your children?

_____

_____

_____

_____

_____

_____

_____

TRUSTING GOD WITH THE FUTURE

SCRIPTURE

"Trust in the Lord with all your heart and lean not on your own understanding…" — Proverbs 3:5 (NIV)

DEVOTIONAL

As a father, you instinctively want to protect your children from pain, disappointment, and failure. You want to shield them from every heartache, danger, and mistake. But the reality is, you won't always be able to. No matter how hard you try or how many precautions you take, there will be moments when your children face challenges that you cannot prevent. This is one of the most difficult aspects of fatherhood: surrendering your children's future to God. It's not easy, but it's an essential act of trust.

Trusting God with your children doesn't mean relinquishing your role as their protector and guide—it means letting go of the illusion of control. You can't control every circumstance or decision in their lives, but you can rest assured that God loves them more deeply than you ever could. Surrendering their future to Him allows you to lead them with peace, knowing that He is ultimately in control, even when things feel uncertain. It's an act of faith that not only frees you but also teaches your children the power of trusting God with their own lives.

PRAYER

Father, I surrender my fears and my hopes for my children. I trust You to guide their future. Teach me to lead them today while trusting You with tomorrow. Amen.

REFLECTION

Are there areas where you find it hard to surrender control over your children's future? How can you take a step of faith today, trusting God with their lives and their well-being? Write a prayer of surrender, asking God to guide your children and help you lead with peace and trust in His plan.

_____
_____
_____
_____
_____
_____
_____

GUARDING YOUR HEART

SCRIPTURE

"Above all else, guard your heart, for everything you do flows from it." — Proverbs 4:23 (NIV)

DEVOTIONAL

A strong father begins with a heart that is guarded and intentional about what it allows in. In the world we live in, there are countless distractions and influences that can easily shape us—through the media we consume, the words we speak, and the habits we form. What you let into your heart and mind impacts not only the man you are becoming but also the way you lead your family. Protecting your heart is an act of responsibility, a choice to be mindful of the influences that shape your thoughts, actions, and emotions.

But guarding your heart is more than just defense—it's about preparation. When your heart is firmly anchored in God, you can fill it with His love, wisdom, and truth. This foundation equips you to pour out life into your home, to love your children well, and to lead with integrity. The more you protect and cultivate your heart, the more you can offer your family the strength, peace, and guidance they need. A father whose heart is aligned with God's will can serve as a constant source of love and direction for his children.

PRAYER

Lord, help me protect my heart from what draws me away from You. Fill it instead with Your wisdom, peace, and strength. Let what flows out of me lead my children closer to You. Amen.

REFLECTION

What are the influences in your life that shape your heart and mind? Are there any areas where you need to be more intentional about guarding your heart? Take a moment to reflect on how you can anchor your heart more deeply in God's truth today, and how that will impact your leadership as a father.

_____

_____

_____

_____

_____

_____

_____

SHOWING AFFECTION WITHOUT APOLOGY

SCRIPTURE

"As a father has compassion on his children, so the Lord has compassion on those who fear him."
— Psalm 103:13 (NIV)

DEVOTIONAL

Your children need more than the basics of provision and protection—they need affection. In the hustle and bustle of life, it's easy to overlook the simple acts of love that can have a profound impact on their hearts. A hug, a kind word, or an encouraging note may seem small, but they carry a depth of meaning that far outweighs any material gift. These moments of tenderness create security and emotional warmth, helping your children feel valued and loved in a way that no material possession can provide.

In a world that often equates strength with toughness, it's important to remember that love is not just about discipline and boundaries—it's also about tenderness. Don't let culture convince you that affection is a sign of weakness. Show your children that love can be both strong and soft. When you embrace them with your arms, speak to them with kind words, and look at them with eyes full of compassion, you reflect the heart of God—a love that is unyielding, yet gentle, and always full of grace.

PRAYER

Father, thank You for Your compassion toward me. Help me show that same tenderness to my children every day. Let them feel Your love through mine. Amen.

REFLECTION

How do you show affection to your children in both big and small ways? Are there moments when you could be more intentional about expressing love through touch, words, or actions? Reflect on how you can create more opportunities for tenderness in your relationship with your children.

_____

_____

_____

_____

_____

_____

_____

THE STRENGTH TO SAY "I'M SORRY"

SCRIPTURE

"Confess your sins to each other and pray for each other so that you may be healed."
— James 5:16a (NIV)

DEVOTIONAL

Apologizing to your children is one of the most powerful things you can do as a father. It shows them that being human means making mistakes, but it also teaches them that failure is not the end of the story. When you humble yourself and say "I'm sorry," you demonstrate that acknowledging your shortcomings is a strength, not a weakness. This act of humility models grace and provides a profound lesson in leadership—showing your children that it's okay to admit when you're wrong and to make amends.

By offering a sincere apology, you invite healing and growth into your relationship with your children. It breaks down walls of pride and opens up the space for deeper connection and trust. When your children see you model grace, they learn that relationships are built on understanding, not perfection. Never underestimate the power of an apology—it is a tool that brings both reconciliation and growth.

PRAYER

Lord, give me the strength to admit when I've been wrong. Help me be quick to apologize and quick to forgive. Make my home a place of healing and honesty. Amen.

REFLECTION

Think about a time when you had to apologize to your children. How did it impact your relationship? Are there any moments where you may need to offer an apology or extend grace to your children today? Reflect on how humility in your leadership strengthens the bond between you and your children.

_____

_____

_____

_____

_____

_____

_____

THE COURAGE TO LEAD DIFFERENTLY

SCRIPTURE

"Do not conform to the pattern of this world, but be transformed by the renewing of your mind."
— Romans 12:2 (NIV)

DEVOTIONAL

Culture often defines fatherhood as a role filled with control, toughness, and emotional distance—but God calls you to a higher standard. You're not meant to follow the world's expectations of what a father should be. Instead, you are called to lead with love, faith, and humility, which might look countercultural in a world that values power and independence. Your role as a father isn't about fitting in, it's about standing out as a reflection of God's heart.

Leading with love and faith might not always look like the world's definition of strength, but it's this kind of leadership that truly transforms a family. When you model humility, grace, and unconditional love, you create an environment where your children can grow spiritually, emotionally, and mentally. This approach to fatherhood shapes not just your children, but your entire family, from the inside out, and leaves a lasting legacy of faith.

PRAYER

God, give me the courage to lead differently. Let me reflect You, not the world. Help me build a home that's shaped by truth, not trends. Amen.

REFLECTION

In what ways do you feel pressure to conform to cultural expectations of fatherhood? How can you lead your family with love, humility, and faith, even when it feels countercultural? Reflect on how standing out in your fatherhood can transform not just your relationship with your children, but your whole family.

_____

_____

_____

_____

_____

_____

_____

_____

_____

EMBRACING THE EVERYDAY

SCRIPTURE

"And whatever you do, whether in word or deed, do it all in the name of the Lord Jesus..."
— Colossians 3:17 (NIV)

DEVOTIONAL

Not every day of fatherhood feels monumental. Some days are messy, routine, or downright exhausting. But even in the mundane moments—whether it's tucking your child in at night, running errands together, or showing up at practice—God sees the significance. These everyday acts, though often overlooked, are shaping your child's sense of security and love. They may not seem epic, but they're foundational.

In God's eyes, the ordinary is often where the sacred is hiding. It's in these simple, repetitive moments that you're building a legacy of faith and trust. Don't underestimate the power of showing up, even when it feels like just another day. These small moments create lasting memories and serve as a constant reminder to your children that you are there for them, in both the big moments and the small ones.

PRAYER

Lord, help me see You in the everyday. Remind me that even the smallest acts of fatherhood can reflect Your love. Give me joy in the simple moments. Amen.

REFLECTION

Think about a recent ordinary day with your child— was there a moment you might have overlooked? How can you intentionally recognize the sacredness in these small, everyday moments? Reflect on the ways your presence, even in the mundane, impacts your child's heart.

_____
_____
_____
_____
_____
_____
_____
_____
_____
_____

TEACHING THROUGH EXAMPLE

SCRIPTURE

"Fathers, do not exasperate your children; instead, bring them up in the training and instruction of the Lord." — Ephesians 6:4 (NIV)

DEVOTIONAL

Your children may not recall every specific lesson or piece of advice you offer, but they will always remember how you lived. The way you interact with them, the choices you make, and the character you display shapes their understanding of God, relationships, and responsibility. Your actions speak louder than words—integrity isn't something that can simply be taught; it's something they'll catch by watching you.

When you model patience, prayerfulness, and honesty, you're teaching them lessons that go beyond what's spoken. Your example provides a living guide for them to follow. This is how lasting lessons are learned—not through lectures or instructions, but through your everyday actions that reflect the values you want them to carry forward.

PRAYER

Father, help me live in a way that points my children to You. Let my actions align with my words, and my life reflect Your truth. Amen.

REFLECTION

Think about the values you want to pass down to your children. How are you currently modeling patience, honesty, and prayerfulness in your daily life? Reflect on one specific way you can show them these traits today, and how that will impact their view of God and relationships.

_____

_____

_____

_____

_____

_____

_____

_____

_____

_____

THE POWER OF BLESSING

SCRIPTURE

"The Lord bless you and keep you; the Lord make his face shine on you and be gracious to you…"
— Numbers 6:24-25 (NIV)

DEVOTIONAL

Your words hold incredible power to shape your children's identity. When you affirm their worth, call out their unique gifts, and speak God's promises over their lives, you're building a foundation of faith, confidence, and security. Each word you speak plants seeds of truth that will grow within them, shaping how they see themselves and the world around them. Your encouragement is a powerful tool that helps them know they are loved, valued, and capable.

Blessing your children isn't just about offering a prayer or special moment—it's about making the choice every day to speak life into their hearts. It's in the simple, everyday words that you build their future, nurturing their sense of purpose and strength. By consistently affirming their value and reminding them of God's faithfulness, you're equipping them to face challenges with confidence and trust in the truth that God has a plan for their lives.

PRAYER

God, help me to bless my children with my words and actions. Let them know they are loved, valued, and called by You. Teach me to speak into their lives with faith. Amen.

REFLECTION

What are some specific ways you can speak blessings over your children today? How can you affirm their worth and remind them of God's promises in everyday moments? Reflect on how your words can shape their identity and build their confidence in God's truth.

_____
_____
_____
_____
_____
_____
_____
_____

HONORING THE MOTHER OF YOUR CHILDREN

SCRIPTURE

"Husbands, love your wives, just as Christ loved the church and gave himself up for her."
— Ephesians 5:25 (NIV)

DEVOTIONAL

One of the most powerful gifts you can give your children is a consistent example of how to love and respect their mother. Whether you are married, co-parenting, or working through a complex relationship, your children are always observing how you speak about her and treat her. Your actions toward her shape their understanding of love, respect, and partnership. Even small moments of kindness, support, and honor leave a lasting impression.

When you choose to honor her in both word and deed, you're not only building trust—you're showing your children what it means to love with integrity. They learn that real love is respectful, patient, and selfless. The way you handle disagreements, extend grace, and speak with kindness teaches them how to build healthy relationships in their own lives. Loving her well is a legacy that blesses generations.

PRAYER

Lord, help me love with Christ-like humility and strength. Teach me to honor the mother of my children with kindness and grace. Let my relationship with her reflect Your heart. Amen.

REFLECTION

How do your words and actions toward your children's mother reflect the love and respect God calls you to show? Are there any areas where you could model that love more intentionally? Reflect on how your treatment of her is shaping your children's understanding of healthy relationships.

_____

_____

_____

_____

_____

_____

_____

_____

WHEN YOU FEEL INADEQUATE

SCRIPTURE

"But he said to me, 'My grace is sufficient for you, for my power is made perfect in weakness.'"
— 2 Corinthians 12:9a (NIV)

DEVOTIONAL

Every dad faces moments of doubt—times when you feel like you're falling short or not measuring up. The truth is, you aren't enough on your own, and that's not a flaw—it's a reminder of your need for God. He never called you to be a perfect father. He simply asks you to be present, faithful, and willing to lean on Him daily. Your presence matters more than perfection, and your willingness to keep showing up, even when you feel inadequate, is powerful.

God's grace is what bridges the gap between your limitations and the high calling of fatherhood. Your weaknesses don't disqualify you; they open the door for His strength to shine through. When you lead with humility and dependence on God, you show your children what real strength looks like—a strength that comes not from self-reliance, but from trusting the One who is always enough.

PRAYER

Father, when I feel like I'm not enough, remind me that Your grace is. Help me rest in Your power and lead from a place of humility and trust. Amen.

REFLECTION

What areas of fatherhood make you feel the most inadequate or overwhelmed? How might God be inviting you to rely on His strength in those places? Reflect on how your dependence on Him can actually become one of the greatest gifts you give your children.

_____
_____
_____
_____
_____
_____
_____
_____
_____

STAYING STEADY IN CHAOS

SCRIPTURE

"He will be the sure foundation for your times, a rich store of salvation and wisdom and knowledge…"
— Isaiah 33:6a (NIV)

DEVOTIONAL

Kids don't just need you to show up in the big moments—they need you to be steady in the everyday ones. Life can be unpredictable and messy, but your consistency gives them a sense of safety. When they know they can count on you, even when everything else feels uncertain, it builds deep trust. Your steady presence becomes a quiet strength that anchors the atmosphere of your home.

Even when storms come—whether emotional, relational, or circumstantial—your calm and grounded response teaches your children where true peace is found. When your heart is anchored in Christ, it naturally flows into how you lead, love, and respond. Your stability doesn't just keep your home steady—it shows your children how to stay rooted when their world feels shaken.

PRAYER

God, be my anchor when life feels overwhelming. Help me bring peace into my home, not chaos. Let my steadiness be a reflection of Your faithfulness. Amen.

REFLECTION

Think about a recent situation where life felt chaotic at home. How did you respond? How might anchoring your heart in Christ help you bring steadiness to your family in future moments of stress or uncertainty? Reflect on what it means to be a calm, consistent presence for your children.

_____
_____
_____
_____
_____
_____
_____
_____
_____
_____

CULTIVATING A GRATEFUL HOME

SCRIPTURE

"Give thanks in all circumstances; for this is God's will for you in Christ Jesus."
— 1 Thessalonians 5:18 (NIV)

DEVOTIONAL

Gratitude is one of the most powerful attitudes you can model for your children. It doesn't mean pretending everything is perfect or ignoring life's struggles—it means choosing to recognize and speak about God's goodness even in the middle of difficulty. When your kids see you give thanks during hard times, they learn that joy isn't based on circumstances, but on trust in a faithful God.

Your words of gratitude shape the atmosphere of your home. They create an environment where contentment, peace, and joy can grow. A dad who consistently gives thanks—whether for small blessings or in the face of trials—teaches his children to be grounded and joyful. Gratitude doesn't just lift your own heart; it lifts the hearts of everyone around you.

PRAYER

Lord, teach me to be thankful in all circumstances. Let my words and actions overflow with gratitude so my home becomes a place of joy and praise. Amen.

REFLECTION

What are three things you're grateful for today—especially in the midst of any current challenges? How can you express that gratitude in front of your children this week? Reflect on how your attitude of thankfulness might shape the tone and atmosphere of your home.

_____

_____

_____

_____

_____

_____

_____

_____

_____

_____

BUILDING LEGACY, NOT JUST MEMORIES

SCRIPTURE

"The righteous lead blameless lives; blessed are their children after them." — Proverbs 20:7 (NIV)

DEVOTIONAL

Anyone can create fun memories—through trips, games, or special moments—but a father who lives with purpose builds something deeper: legacy. A legacy isn't just about what you do; it's about who you are. When your life is marked by faith, integrity, and unconditional love, you're planting seeds that grow long after the moment has passed. These lasting values shape the hearts of your children and set the foundation for future generations.

While vacations and laughter are meaningful, it's your quiet consistency, your unseen sacrifices, and your daily choices that tell the real story. Who you are when no one's watching—how you pray, how you treat others, how you pursue God—writes a legacy that will outlive you. Ask yourself: what story is your life telling, and how do you want your children to remember it?

PRAYER

God, help me live in a way that leaves a legacy of love and faith. Let my character speak louder than my words. May my life point my children to You. Amen.

REFLECTION

What kind of legacy do you want to leave for your children? Are there specific values or habits you hope they carry into their own lives and families? Reflect on how your daily choices—seen and unseen—are shaping that legacy right now.

_____
_____
_____
_____
_____
_____
_____
_____
_____
_____
_____
_____
_____

LEANING INTO GOD'S STRENGTH

SCRIPTURE

"The Lord gives strength to his people; the Lord blesses his people with peace." — Psalm 29:11 (NIV)

DEVOTIONAL

Fatherhood requires a deep reservoir of strength—emotionally to guide with wisdom, spiritually to lead with integrity, and physically to show up day after day. The world often tells dads to tough it out, to handle everything on their own, and to never show weakness. But God offers a different definition of strength. He invites you to lean into Him, to draw from His power rather than your own. True strength begins with surrender, not self-reliance.

You were never meant to carry the weight of fatherhood alone. When you stay connected to God—through prayer, Scripture, and dependence on His Spirit—His strength becomes your foundation. In His presence, you find peace that calms the chaos and power that sustains you through every challenge. You don't have to be the strongest in your home—you just need to stay close to the One who is.

PRAYER

Lord, I need Your strength today. Remind me that I don't have to carry everything on my own. Fill me with Your peace as I lean into Your power. Amen.

REFLECTION

Where are you currently trying to carry the weight of fatherhood on your own? What would it look like to surrender that area to God and rely on His strength instead of yours? Write a prayer asking God to help you lead from a place of dependence, not pressure.

_____
_____
_____
_____
_____
_____
_____
_____
_____
_____
_____
_____

WHEN PATIENCE RUNS THIN

SCRIPTURE

"Be completely humble and gentle; be patient, bearing with one another in love."
— Ephesians 4:2 (NIV)

DEVOTIONAL

There will be days when your kids push every button and stretch your patience thin. But patience isn't weakness—it's a powerful, active choice. It's the discipline of holding your peace when emotions run high, and choosing to respond rather than react. True patience requires strength, humility, and the help of the Holy Spirit. It's not always easy, but it's always worth it.

Every moment you respond with patience is a moment your children see what love looks like under pressure. It shows them that love isn't just a feeling—it's a commitment to kindness, even when it's hard. Your calm presence teaches them emotional control, grace, and forgiveness. In those testing moments, you're not just managing behavior—you're shaping hearts.

PRAYER

Father, when my patience is stretched thin, fill me with Your Spirit. Help me respond with gentleness and love, even when it's hard. Let my tone teach as much as my words. Amen.

REFLECTION

Think about a recent moment when your patience was tested as a dad. How did you respond, and what might you do differently next time with God's help? Ask the Lord to grow patience in you, and reflect on how your reactions can become powerful lessons in grace for your children.

_____

_____

_____

_____

_____

_____

_____

_____

_____

CHOOSING PRESENCE OVER PERFECTION

SCRIPTURE

"Better a dry crust with peace and quiet than a house full of feasting, with strife."
— Proverbs 17:1 (NIV)

DEVOTIONAL

Your kids aren't looking for perfection—they're looking for you. They need a dad who shows up, who listens, who makes time even when life is busy. You might stumble over your words, miss a few plans, or feel unsure of what to do, but your consistent presence offers more security than any grand gesture. Being there, day in and day out, is what truly shapes their sense of love and belonging.

In a world that glorifies hustle and performance, it's easy to feel like you're not doing enough. But don't let the pressure to get everything right steal the sacred moments of simply being with your children. A shared laugh, an unhurried meal, or a quiet bedtime chat can mean more than any big event. Presence is the real gift—it's where connection, love, and legacy are formed.

PRAYER

God, help me to value presence over perfection. Let me slow down and be fully engaged with the people You've entrusted to me. Amen.

REFLECTION

Think about the last meaningful moment you shared with your child—what made it special? Are there any distractions or pressures keeping you from being fully present right now? Write down one small way you can be more present with your child this week, and ask God to help you treasure those moments.

_____
_____
_____
_____
_____
_____
_____
_____
_____

STRENGTH THROUGH SURRENDER

SCRIPTURE

"Humble yourselves, therefore, under God's mighty hand, that he may lift you up in due time."
— 1 Peter 5:6 (NIV)

DEVOTIONAL

In God's kingdom, strength doesn't come from control—it comes from surrender. While the world tells you to take charge and rely on your own strength, God invites you to lay down your pride, your plans, and your grip on every outcome. Surrender isn't giving up; it's giving over. It's trusting that God's way is better, even when it's not the easiest or most obvious path.

A strong father isn't the one who has all the answers or carries every burden alone. True strength is found in daily dependence on God—kneeling in prayer, seeking wisdom, and allowing Him to lead you as you lead your family. Your willingness to surrender sets the tone for your home and shows your children that strength and humility can—and should—go hand in hand.

PRAYER

Lord, I surrender my need to control and my desire to prove myself. Fill me with Your strength as I trust Your ways over mine. Amen.

REFLECTION

What area of your life or fatherhood are you still trying to control on your own? What fears or pressures are making it hard to fully surrender? Take a few moments to honestly bring those to God in prayer, and ask Him to help you trust His strength over your own.

_____

_____

_____

_____

_____

_____

_____

_____

_____

_____

SPEAKING LIFE

SCRIPTURE

"The tongue has the power of life and death..."
— Proverbs 18:21a (NIV)

DEVOTIONAL

Your words carry incredible weight in the lives of your children. Every phrase, every tone, every moment of communication has the power to either build them up or tear them down. When you speak with intention—offering encouragement, truth, and love—you're planting seeds that can grow into confidence, faith, and resilience. Your voice becomes one of the first and most influential guides your children will carry with them throughout their lives.

Being mindful of how you speak isn't just about avoiding harsh words; it's about actively choosing to be a source of strength and blessing. Your words can become a lasting soundtrack in your children's hearts, reminding them of their worth and God's love. When you speak life into them daily, you help shape their identity in powerful and positive ways that echo far beyond childhood.

PRAYER

God, help me use my words wisely. Let them be filled with grace, truth, and encouragement. Teach me to speak life into my children every single day. Amen.

REFLECTION

Think about the words you most often speak to your children. Are they mostly encouraging, truthful, and loving? Reflect on a time when your words had a positive impact on them. What intentional changes can you make to ensure your words consistently build up and bless your kids?

_____
_____
_____
_____
_____
_____
_____
_____
_____
_____
_____

LIVING WITH INTEGRITY

SCRIPTURE

"The integrity of the upright guides them, but the unfaithful are destroyed by their duplicity."
— Proverbs 11:3 (NIV)

DEVOTIONAL

Integrity is about being consistent in who you are—whether you're in the spotlight or alone. It means choosing honesty even when no one else is around to witness, keeping your promises no matter the cost, and doing what's right even when it's difficult or inconvenient. This kind of character doesn't develop overnight; it's shaped by daily decisions to live authentically and faithfully.

When your children observe you living with integrity, you provide them with a powerful example and a moral compass that will guide them throughout their lives. Your actions teach them the importance of trustworthiness and honor, helping them understand that true strength comes from doing what is right, not what is easy. This legacy of integrity is one of the most valuable gifts you can leave behind.

PRAYER

Lord, shape my character from the inside out. Help me walk in integrity so my children see what it looks like to follow You in every area of life. Amen.

REFLECTION

Reflect on a recent situation where you had the choice to act with integrity or take an easier path. How did you respond? Are there areas in your life where you struggle to be consistent in private and public? Write a prayer asking God to strengthen your commitment to live with integrity every day.

___
___
___
___
___
___
___
___
___
___

TEACHING FORGIVENESS

SCRIPTURE

"Be kind and compassionate to one another, forgiving each other, just as in Christ God forgave you." — Ephesians 4:32 (NIV)

DEVOTIONAL

Your children learn the heart of forgiveness not just through words, but by watching how you practice it in real life. When you forgive their mistakes with grace, ask for their forgiveness when you fall short, or navigate conflicts with humility and love in your marriage, you provide them with a living example of God's mercy. These moments teach them that forgiveness is not just an idea—it's a powerful choice that brings healing and restoration.

Forgiveness doesn't mean overlooking or excusing wrongs. Instead, it's the deliberate decision to release bitterness and choose love, even when it's hard. By modeling this kind of grace, you help your children understand that relationships can be mended and hearts can be renewed. Your example shows them that forgiveness is a path to freedom and peace, both in their own lives and in the family they build one day.

PRAYER

Lord, help me lead my family with a heart full of compassion. Teach me to forgive quickly and fully, just as You have forgiven me. Amen.

REFLECTION

Think about a time when you struggled to forgive someone—maybe even a family member. What made forgiveness difficult? How did God's grace help you (or how could it help you) choose love over bitterness? Write a prayer asking God to soften your heart and give you the strength to forgive as He forgives.

_____
_____
_____
_____
_____
_____
_____
_____
_____
_____

BEING SLOW TO ANGER

SCRIPTURE

"Everyone should be quick to listen, slow to speak and slow to become angry." — James 1:19 (NIV)

DEVOTIONAL

Anger is a natural emotion that everyone experiences, but it doesn't have to control your reactions—especially as a father. When faced with frustration or conflict, you hold the power to either escalate tensions or bring calm and peace. Your response sets the tone for your home, influencing how your children learn to handle their own emotions and challenges. Choosing patience over anger is a way to lead with wisdom and love.

By intentionally choosing to listen and respond calmly, you create a safe and nurturing environment where your kids feel understood and valued. Your steady presence in moments of difficulty teaches them that it's possible to face challenges without losing control. This kind of leadership fosters trust and emotional security, helping your children grow into confident, resilient individuals.

PRAYER

God, give me wisdom in moments of frustration. Teach me to pause, listen, and respond with grace. Help me reflect Your peace, even under pressure. Amen.

REFLECTION

Recall a recent moment when you felt anger rising in a parenting situation. How did you respond? What might you do differently next time to bring calm instead of tension? Write a prayer asking God to help you cultivate patience and a peaceful spirit in your home.

_____

_____

_____

_____

_____

_____

_____

_____

_____

_____

CELEBRATING THE WINS

SCRIPTURE

"Rejoice with those who rejoice..."
— Romans 12:15a (NIV)

DEVOTIONAL

Celebrating the small victories in your child's life—whether it's taking their first steps, earning good grades, showing kindness, or simply trying their best—can have a powerful impact on their confidence and self-worth. These everyday moments are the building blocks of their identity and resilience. When you take time to notice and celebrate them, you send a clear message that their efforts matter, regardless of the outcome.

As a father, your encouragement becomes a source of strength and motivation for your children. Instead of waiting for big accomplishments to offer praise, choose to celebrate the little wins along the way. This consistent affirmation nurtures a positive spirit in your child and helps them understand that they are valued simply for who they are, not just what they achieve. Your joyful cheers can inspire them to keep growing and trying with confidence.

PRAYER

Lord, help me notice and celebrate the good in my children. Let me be their biggest encourager, always pointing them back to Your joy and purpose. Amen.

REFLECTION

Think about the last time you praised your child. Was it for a big achievement or a small, everyday victory? How might celebrating more of the little moments impact your child's confidence and your relationship? Write down three small victories you can celebrate with your child this week and plan how you'll cheer them on.

_____
_____
_____
_____
_____
_____
_____
_____
_____

PRAYING FOR YOUR CHILDREN

SCRIPTURE

"The prayer of a righteous person is powerful and effective." — James 5:16b (NIV)

DEVOTIONAL

One of the most powerful and profound acts of fatherhood is prayer. While you may not always be able to fix every challenge or solve every problem your children face, you have the incredible privilege of lifting them up to the One who can. Prayer invites God's protection, guidance, and blessings into their lives in a way nothing else can. By praying specifically for their safety, their future, their hearts, and their friendships, you are partnering with God to shape their journey in faith and grace.

Praying over your children aloud not only connects you with God but also allows your kids to hear your voice interceding for them. This becomes a beautiful and tangible expression of your love and faith, reminding them that they are deeply cared for and never alone. Your prayers before the throne of God plant seeds of hope and strength that will grow and carry them through life's ups and downs.

PRAYER

Father, thank You for the gift of my children. I lift them to You today—guide them, protect them, and draw them close to You. Help me be faithful in prayer, trusting You with every detail of their lives. Amen.

REFLECTION

How often do you pray aloud for your children? Reflect on a specific time when you felt God's peace or guidance as you prayed for them. What new ways can you incorporate prayer into your daily routine as a father? Write a prayer asking God to help you be faithful in lifting your children before Him.

___
___
___
___
___
___
___
___
___

FINDING REST IN GOD

SCRIPTURE

"Come to me, all you who are weary and burdened, and I will give you rest." — Matthew 11:28 (NIV)

DEVOTIONAL

Being a dad is one of the most rewarding roles you can have, but it's also incredibly demanding and, at times, exhausting. In a culture that often praises nonstop hustle and productivity, taking time to rest can feel like falling behind or showing weakness. Yet, the truth is that rest is not just a luxury—it's a vital part of God's design for your strength and well-being. When you resist the pressure to do it all on your own and allow yourself to pause, you're honoring the rhythm God intended for life.

Resting in God means more than just physical breaks—it's a spiritual practice of trusting Him with the weight of fatherhood. When you slow down and rest in His presence, you're reminded that you are never carrying the responsibility alone. God's strength supports you, His peace refreshes you, and His presence surrounds you. Embracing rest recharges your heart and equips you to lead your family with renewed energy and grace.

PRAYER

Lord, I bring You my exhaustion, my burdens, and my striving. Help me find true rest in You. Restore my strength so I can keep leading well. Amen.

REFLECTION

When was the last time you truly rested—body, mind, and spirit? Reflect on how rest affects your ability to lead and love your family. What barriers keep you from resting well? Write a prayer asking God to help you embrace His rhythm of rest and find strength in Him.

_____
_____
_____
_____
_____
_____
_____
_____
_____
_____
_____

MODELING SERVANT LEADERSHIP

SCRIPTURE

"Whoever wants to become great among you must be your servant." — Matthew 20:26b (NIV)

DEVOTIONAL

The world often measures leadership by power, authority, and control. But Jesus turned that idea upside down by showing that true leadership is found in serving others with humility and love. As a father, the way you lead your family isn't by commanding from a distance, but by stepping in with a willing heart—whether it's washing dishes, helping with homework, or simply showing up when it's inconvenient. These acts of service may seem small or unnoticed, but they carry tremendous weight in teaching your children what real leadership looks like.

When you lead through service, you mirror the example Jesus gave us, demonstrating that strength is found not in domination but in selflessness. This kind of leadership shapes your children's hearts more deeply than words ever could, pointing them toward Christ's example of love and humility. By serving your family, you build a legacy of compassion and grace that will influence generations to come.

PRAYER

Jesus, You served with humility and love. Help me lead my family in the same way—not with pride, but with compassion and sacrifice. Amen.

REFLECTION

Reflect on a recent time when you led your family by serving rather than directing. How did that impact your relationship with your children? What small acts of service can you intentionally incorporate into your daily routine to model Christ-like leadership? Write down one step you can take this week to lead through serving.

_____

_____

_____

_____

_____

_____

_____

_____

TEACHING YOUR KIDS TO TRUST GOD

SCRIPTURE

"Trust in the Lord with all your heart and lean not on your own understanding." — Proverbs 3:5 (NIV)

DEVOTIONAL

Trust isn't something children learn just by hearing about it—it's something they absorb by watching how you live your faith. When your kids see you turn to God in prayer before making decisions, rely on Him during difficult seasons, and remain faithful even when life feels uncertain, they witness a living example of trust in action. Your everyday dependence on God becomes the foundation upon which their own faith can grow.

By modeling this kind of trust, you're doing more than teaching a concept—you're showing your children how to trust with their whole hearts. They learn that faith isn't about having all the answers, but about leaning on God's wisdom and grace when the path isn't clear. Your example becomes a powerful guide that helps them build their own enduring relationship with God.

PRAYER

Lord, help me model what it looks like to trust You wholeheartedly. Let my life be a testimony my children can follow as they learn to walk in faith. Amen.

REFLECTION

Think about a recent situation where you relied on God's guidance in a difficult decision or challenge. How did your response demonstrate trust to your children? In what ways can you more openly model leaning on God in front of your family? Write a prayer asking God to help you be a living example of faith and trust.

_____
_____
_____
_____
_____
_____
_____
_____
_____

CORRECTING WITH GRACE

SCRIPTURE

"The Lord disciplines those he loves…"
— Hebrews 12:6a (NIV)

DEVOTIONAL

Discipline isn't about punishment or control—it's about love that provides clear direction. As a father, your role is to gently guide your children back to the right path when they stray, offering both firmness and compassion. Discipline helps shape their character and teaches important life lessons, but it should always come from a place of care and concern, not frustration or anger.

True correction flows from a heart full of love and a desire to see your children grow into the people God created them to be. It balances grace with truth—offering forgiveness and understanding while holding firm to boundaries. When discipline is rooted in this balance, it becomes a powerful tool to nurture your child's growth and reflect God's loving guidance.

PRAYER

Father, teach me to correct my children in love, not frustration. Let my discipline be an act of grace that helps them grow into who You've called them to be. Amen.

REFLECTION

Reflect on how you currently approach discipline with your children. Are your corrections more often motivated by frustration or by love and a desire to guide? Write about ways you can balance grace and truth in your discipline. Pray for God's wisdom and patience to lead your family with a loving, steady heart.

_____

_____

_____

_____

_____

_____

_____

_____

_____

_____

POINTING TO PURPOSE

SCRIPTURE

"For we are God's handiwork, created in Christ Jesus to do good works..." — Ephesians 2:10a (NIV)

DEVOTIONAL

Every child has a deep desire to know that their life truly matters—that they were created with intention and value. As a father, you hold a powerful role in affirming this truth. You have the privilege of helping your children recognize the unique gifts and talents God has placed within them. When you take the time to notice, encourage, and nurture their strengths, you are planting seeds of confidence and purpose in their hearts.

By speaking life into their dreams and consistently reminding them that they were made on purpose for a purpose, you help shape their identity and destiny. Your words become a foundation that supports them through challenges and inspires them to step boldly into the calling God has for their lives. This kind of encouragement is one of the greatest gifts a father can give.

PRAYER

God, help me see and speak the purpose You've placed in my children. Give me wisdom to nurture their gifts and guide them toward Your plans. Amen.

REFLECTION

Take some time to reflect on your child's unique gifts and talents. How have you encouraged them to explore these gifts? Write down specific ways you can speak life and purpose into your child's heart this week. Pray for God to reveal your child's potential and for wisdom to nurture their calling.

_____
_____
_____
_____
_____
_____
_____
_____
_____
_____
_____

LIVING A LEGACY OF FAITH

SCRIPTURE

"But as for me and my household, we will serve the Lord." — Joshua 24:15b (NIV)

DEVOTIONAL

Faith isn't merely a topic for conversation or a set of beliefs—it's a way of life. As a father, the way you live out your faith in everyday moments speaks louder than words. Every prayer you lift up, every time you open the Bible to seek wisdom, and every choice to respond with grace instead of frustration is a brick laid in the foundation of your family's spiritual journey. Your daily walk with God becomes a living example that your children can see and follow.

One day, your children will look back and remember not just what you said about faith, but how you lived it—through both the big moments and the ordinary ones. When they see a father who truly walks with God, it leaves a legacy that goes beyond your lifetime. This kind of faith-filled legacy shapes hearts, strengthens futures, and honors God in the most lasting way.

PRAYER

Lord, let my life be a living testimony of Your goodness. Help me build a legacy of faith that draws my children closer to You with every step I take. Amen.

REFLECTION

Reflect on how your daily actions and choices reflect your faith. In what ways are you living out your belief in front of your children? Write about one practical step you can take this week to deepen your walk with God and strengthen the spiritual legacy you're building for your family.

_____

_____

_____

_____

_____

_____

_____

_____

_____

_____

FATHERING THROUGH FAILURE

SCRIPTURE

"Though he may stumble, he will not fall, for the Lord upholds him with his hand." — Psalm 37:24 (NIV)

DEVOTIONAL

You're going to make mistakes—that's part of being human and part of being a dad. There will be times when you miss important moments, say the wrong thing, or react in ways you later wish you could take back. But these failures don't define or disqualify you as a father. Instead, they offer powerful opportunities for growth and humility, reminding you of your ongoing need for God's guidance and grace.

When you openly admit your mistakes and show your children how to learn from them, you teach them invaluable lessons about resilience and forgiveness. Your willingness to grow and rely on God sets a real-life example that perfection isn't the goal—progress and grace are. This transparency helps your children understand that mistakes aren't the end but stepping stones on the path of life and faith.

PRAYER

Father, thank You that Your grace covers my failures. Teach me to grow through them, and help me model humility and perseverance for my children. Amen.

REFLECTION

Think about a recent mistake or moment you wish you had handled differently as a father. How did you respond, and what did you learn from it? Write about how you can model humility and resilience to your children by openly admitting your mistakes and relying on God's grace. What steps can you take to grow stronger in your role as a dad?

_____
_____
_____
_____
_____
_____
_____
_____
_____

LOVING THEIR MOM WELL

SCRIPTURE

"Husbands, love your wives, just as Christ loved the church and gave himself up for her."
— Ephesians 5:25 (NIV)

DEVOTIONAL

One of the most powerful gifts you can give your children is to love their mother well. Whether you're married, divorced, or widowed, the way you honor, respect, and care for her leaves a lasting imprint on their hearts. Your actions speak louder than words, showing your children what healthy relationships look like and teaching them about kindness, respect, and commitment.

For your sons, your love models what it means to be a godly leader—someone who leads with humility, strength, and respect. For your daughters, your love paints a picture of the kind of love they deserve—one that is patient, selfless, and steadfast. By loving their mother well, you're shaping how they will love others and how they will expect to be loved in return.

PRAYER

Father, thank You that Your grace covers my failures. Teach me to grow through them, and help me model humility and perseverance for my children. Amen.

REFLECTION

Reflect on the ways you currently show love and respect to your children's mother. How do your actions and words model healthy love for your kids? Are there areas where you feel God is calling you to grow in honoring her more fully? Write about practical steps you can take to demonstrate love that leaves a lasting legacy for your children.

_____
_____
_____
_____
_____
_____
_____
_____

WHEN YOU FEEL ALONE

SCRIPTURE

"Never will I leave you; never will I forsake you."
— Hebrews 13:5b (NIV)

DEVOTIONAL

There will be moments in fatherhood that feel isolating—times when the weight of responsibility feels heavy, and it seems like no one truly understands the challenges you face. Those moments can be lonely and overwhelming, making you question if you have the strength to keep going. But in those very times, it's important to remember that you are never truly alone.

God sees your struggles, hears your prayers, and walks closely beside you every step of the way. He is your constant source of strength in the quiet moments and your uplifting presence when no one else is watching. Fathering is a journey you don't take alone—your Heavenly Father is always at your side, ready to guide, comfort, and empower you to lead well.

PRAYER

Lord, in moments of loneliness, remind me You are near. Let Your presence fill every empty space and give me strength to keep going. Amen.

REFLECTION

Think about a time recently when fatherhood felt especially heavy or isolating. How did you respond in that moment? Take a moment to write a prayer inviting God's presence into those hard places. How can you remind yourself daily that you're never alone, even when the weight feels overwhelming? What practical steps can you take to lean more on God's strength in your fathering journey?

_____
_____
_____
_____
_____
_____
_____
_____
_____

LEADING WITH COURAGE

SCRIPTURE

"Have I not commanded you? Be strong and courageous. Do not be afraid… for the Lord your God will be with you wherever you go."
— Joshua 1:9 (NIV)

DEVOTIONAL

Courage doesn't mean the absence of fear—it means stepping forward and doing what's right even when fear is present. As a father, you will face moments that require tough decisions, times when standing up for truth feels risky, and seasons filled with uncertainty. It's natural to feel afraid, but true courage is moving forward despite those fears, trusting that God is with you every step of the way.

You are never alone in these moments. God's presence is your source of strength and courage, empowering you to lead with boldness and integrity. Your faith not only sustains you but also inspires your family to be brave and steadfast. By leaning on God, your courage becomes a powerful example that encourages your children to face life's challenges with confidence and hope.

PRAYER

God, give me strength and courage to lead with integrity and faith. Let my children see that trusting You is the bravest thing we can do. Amen.

REFLECTION

Reflect on a recent situation where fear tried to hold you back from doing what you knew was right as a father. How did you respond? Write about the ways God helped you find courage in that moment or how you wish you had leaned on Him more. What specific steps can you take to rely on God's presence next time you face uncertainty or difficult decisions?

_____

_____

_____

_____

_____

_____

_____

_____

_____

_____

BECOMING A SAFE PLACE

SCRIPTURE

"The Lord is a refuge for the oppressed, a stronghold in times of trouble." — Psalm 9:9 (NIV)

DEVOTIONAL

A strong father isn't just someone who protects from harm—he's a safe place where his children feel secure and loved. He becomes the person they run to in moments of joy and in times of tears, the one they trust with their questions, fears, and confessions. By creating a home where hearts can open freely, he fosters an environment of trust and emotional safety.

When honesty is met with compassion instead of judgment, children learn that they can be real and vulnerable without fear. Your arms, open and welcoming, can mirror the refuge your Heavenly Father offers—steady, loving, and unwavering. In this safe space, your children will grow confident in God's love and your steadfast presence.

PRAYER

Lord, make me a safe place for my children. Help me listen with love, respond with grace, and always point them back to You. Amen.

REFLECTION

Reflect on the ways you create a safe and loving environment for your children. How do you respond when they come to you with their fears, questions, or mistakes? What steps can you take to make your home an even safer place for open and honest communication? Write about how you see God's refuge reflected in your role as a father.

_____
_____
_____
_____
_____
_____
_____
_____
_____

EMBRACING THE EVERYDAY

SCRIPTURE

"Whatever you do, work at it with all your heart, as working for the Lord…" — Colossians 3:23 (NIV)

DEVOTIONAL

Fatherhood often unfolds in the quiet rhythms of everyday life—packing lunches, driving to practices, fixing broken things around the house. These tasks may seem ordinary or even tedious, but they hold incredible value when done with love and intention. Each small act is a way to show your children that they matter and that you are there for them, building a foundation of trust and security.

Don't overlook the beauty in these everyday moments. They are the threads that, over time, weave a rich tapestry of legacy and love in your children's lives. What might seem mundane now becomes the lasting fabric of your family's story—a story defined by faithfulness, presence, and a father's steady love.

PRAYER

God, help me see the value in the small things. Let me serve my family with joy, knowing that You are in every moment. Amen.

REFLECTION

What everyday moments in your fatherhood do you often overlook? How can you bring more intentional love and presence into those simple tasks today?

_____
_____
_____
_____
_____
_____
_____
_____
_____
_____
_____
_____
_____

YOUR STRENGTH COMES FROM HIM

SCRIPTURE

"I can do all this through him who gives me strength."
— Philippians 4:13 (NIV)

DEVOTIONAL

You weren't called to fatherhood to rely on your own strength or wisdom. The journey is too big, too important, and too challenging to carry alone. Instead, you were called to lean on God's power and grace every step of the way. When you feel weak, tired, or uncertain, remember that His strength is made perfect in your weakness. You don't have to have all the answers—He does.

On the hardest days, when doubt or exhaustion creep in, God's presence is your constant source of hope and courage. You are never alone or ill-equipped for this calling. You are chosen, empowered, and lovingly held by a Father who never fails or forsakes you. Trust Him, and lean into the strength that never runs dry.

PRAYER

Father, thank You for choosing me to be a dad. On the hard days and the joyful ones, let me always find my strength in You. Amen.

REFLECTION

When have you felt weak or overwhelmed as a father? How can you intentionally lean on God's strength in those moments? Write about a time you experienced God's power helping you through a difficult day or decision.

_____
_____
_____
_____
_____
_____
_____
_____
_____
_____
_____
_____

CLOSING REFLECTION & BLESSING

As you journey through the highs and lows of fatherhood, remember that you are never alone. God walks beside you every step of the way, offering strength when you're weak and wisdom when you're unsure. The heart of a father is shaped not by perfection, but by perseverance and love rooted in Christ. Your daily choices—how you love, serve, and lead—have eternal significance. Even when you feel small or inadequate, God is working through you to build a legacy of faith that will impact generations.

Take comfort in knowing that your efforts matter. The seemingly ordinary moments of patience, grace, and presence are threads woven into a beautiful tapestry of fatherhood. Trust God's promise that He will complete the good work He has begun in you. Keep your heart anchored in Him, and lead with confidence, hope, and a steadfast spirit.

May the Lord bless you and keep you, Father. May His strength uphold you when you feel weary, and His wisdom guide your every step. May His love overflow in your heart, pouring out into your family with grace and patience. May you lead with humility and courage, always pointing your children to the unfailing love of Christ. And may you know, deeply and surely, that you are enough—not because of who you are, but because of *whose* you are. Amen.

ABOUT THE AUTHOR

Rebecca graduated from Malone College in 2008 with a Bachelor's degree in Youth Ministry. She started writing & illustrating in 2013, about her dog Pookie, when she wanted a fun and wholesome story for her nieces and nephews, some of which were learning to read. She plans to keep up her series and write others. In 2019, she launched a publishing and entertainment company to help kids explore and nurture their creative side through books, tv shows, and art classes.

Along with *The Adventures of Pookie* children's book series, she is the illustrator of her sister, Megan Yee's books in the God's Books series. She is also the author of the personal development book *The Creative Minds Guide to Success*. She travels full time in a 5th wheel RV with her husband Eric, and their dog, Bailey, for his job as a Journeyman Lineman and writes about their adventures along the way.

CHECK OUT MORE

AdventuresOfPookie.com

Books

Shows

Classes

www.ingramcontent.com/pod-product-compliance
Lightning Source LLC
Chambersburg PA
CBHW071145090426
42736CB00012B/2226